Can I tell you about Stuttering?

D0064315

Can I tell you about...?

The "Can I tell you about...?" series offers simple introductions to a range of limiting conditions. Friendly characters invite readers to learn about their experiences of living with a particular condition and how they would like to be helped and supported. These books serve as excellent starting points for family and classroom discussions.

Other subjects covered in the "Can I tell you about...?" series

ADHD

Asperger Syndrome

Asthma

Dementia

Dyslexia

Epilepsy

OCD

Parkinson's Disease

Selective Mutism

Can I tell you about Stuttering?

A guide for friends, family, and professionals

SUE COTTRELL
Illustrated by Sophie Khan

Jessica Kingsley *Publishers*
London and Philadelphia

First published in 2013
by Jessica Kingsley Publishers
116 Pentonville Road
London N1 9JB, UK
and
400 Market Street, Suite 400
Philadelphia, PA 19106, USA

www.jkp.com

Library of Congress Cataloging in Publication Data
Cottrell, Sue, 1965-
Can I tell you about stuttering? : a guide for friends, family and
professionals / Sue Cottrell ; illustrated by Sophie Khan.
pages cm
Audience: 7+
ISBN 978-1-84905-435-5 (alk. paper)
1. Stuttering in children--Juvenile literature. 2. Stuttering--Juvenile
literature. 3. Language disorders in children--Juvenile literature. 4.
Language disorders--Juvenile literature. I. Khan, Sophie, illustrator. II. Title.
RJ496.S7C663 2013
618.92'8554--dc23
2013010985

British Library Cataloguing in Publication Data
A CIP catalogue record for this book is available from the British Library

ISBN 978 1 84905 435 5
eISBN 978 0 85700 827 5

Printed and bound in Great Britain by Bell & Bain Ltd, Glasgow

"There are no shortcuts to any
place worth going." (Anon)

This book is dedicated to my son Lloyd, and
to all the people who have helped him on his
journey to become a more confident speaker.

Contents

Acknowledgements

I would like to thank Gareth Gates for speaking openly about his stutter, and enabling me to find out how to help my son, Lloyd, a fellow stutterer. The techniques used by Gareth stem from the McGuire Programme, a world-wide organization run by people who stutter for people who stutter.

While supporting my son throughout his recovery, I have met and been inspired by hundreds of stutterers. Each has his or her own story, but all share the same intense fear of speaking. I am a fluent speaker, and have been humbled by the courage, determination, and perseverance shown by stutterers on their journey to recovery. Many have turned a negative into a positive by overcoming their stutter, then supporting and coaching others.

I commend the work of the McGuire Programme, and would like to offer a huge thank you to all the stutterers in recovery who have supported—and continue to support—Lloyd on his journey.

Introduction

This book has been written to help everyone gain a better understanding of stuttering:

- Children and young people can read about the challenges facing stutterers. The book explains what stuttering is, how it feels to have a stutter, and how to help.

- It is also a useful, friendly book to share with children who stutter to help them understand and talk about how it affects them. It may also help older children who are recovering from a stutter to talk about their past and present experiences.

- And of course adults can learn a lot about stuttering too!

Stuttering affects people all over the world, but every stutterer is an individual and everyone's stutter is different. Not all the ideas presented in this book will fit every child.

"Some people call it stuttering. Others call it stammering. I'd like to tell you what it is, what it feels like, and how you might help me—if you want to."

"You can't see that I have a stutter. I look like most other boys. But you might notice things about me that are a bit different. This is because a stutter can make me behave and talk a bit differently from the way you might expect. Like everyone else, people with stutters are individuals, and stuttering affects each person a bit differently. So other children with stutters will be like me in lots of ways, but not exactly the same.

Having a stutter means that I have difficulty speaking. Sometimes I'm fine, and you wouldn't think I had a problem. But other times, I get anxious and the words don't come out as I want them to.

You may have noticed that sometimes I get stuck when I'm speaking. I open my mouth, but no words come out. Quite often, I repeat a word or the first sound of a word, and my face looks a bit strange. I used to blink a lot when I was trying to say a word, but now I tend to slap my leg. I know what I want to say. And I know how I'd like it to sound. But as soon as I open my mouth, it all gets blocked up.

I don't understand why I have a stutter, or how it all started. My mom says that when I was small, I used to speak very quickly and quietly. Apparently, lots of people struggled to understand what I was saying, especially if they didn't know me well. I started to stutter occasionally when I was about seven or eight, and recently things have become worse."

"I often get stuck saying my name, Harry."

"When I open my mouth to say my name, my jaw seems to freeze up and no sound comes out. Other words beginning with the letter h are also difficult for me.

It's not my fault that I stutter. I used to blame my brother, Peter, because he's got a stutter too. But I understand now that you can't catch a stutter like you catch a cold. One day, I heard my mom telling the neighbor that she felt really guilty about my stutter and was worried it was her fault in some way. Since then, she's read lots of books about stuttering and knows it's not her fault. I've heard it's to do with my genes.

I'm 11 now and in my last year at elementary school. Everyone there used to think I was really shy and quiet, because I didn't talk much, but they understand now that it's because of my stutter.

Some situations are harder than others. School can be really tricky. When the teacher asks a question, I'd rather not put my hand up because then I'd have to speak in front of the class. I'm quite bright and usually know the answer, but I'd rather people think I don't know the answer than watch me struggle and stutter.

When the teacher speaks to me directly, some children in the class turn round to look at me. The teacher tells them not to, but one or two still do. It's the same when I want to ask the teacher a question."

"My mom and I went to see the teacher after school, and the teacher asked me if there was anything she could do to help."

"I know I need to practice speaking, but I don't like being put on the spot. I suggested to the teacher that when we read aloud in class, it would be good if I could go first, as the pressure builds up and up when I'm waiting for my turn. I also suggested that when the teacher asks me a question, it would help if I had more time to think.

My teacher is really kind and asked my mom if she could think of any other ways to boost my confidence in school. I said that I'd like to have a small speaking part in the summer play. This really surprised my teacher—and my mom, I think. I wouldn't want the stress of a main part, but perhaps I could be one of the narrators.

Mom gives me masses of encouragement and is always telling me that I can do it—whatever it is! This makes me feel more confident, which is good, because when I'm feeling confident, I don't stutter so much. Knowing that other people believe in me helps me to believe in myself.

My teacher wrote down all of our ideas to show the other teachers and teaching assistants."

"Some days are much better than others. I don't stutter at all when I speak with my baby cousin."

"My cousin is two and a half, and loves to play with soft toys. Sometimes I make up stories about her toys and use different voices for the goodies and baddies. This makes her giggle, and makes me feel happy too.

I also feel happy when I sing because I don't stutter then either. My mom says this is because singing uses a different part of the brain from speaking. She's probably right, but I also think it's something to do with knowing the words. Things generally flow more easily when I don't have to think too hard about what to say.

When I joined the Scouts, I learnt the scout promise off by heart, but I still worried about saying it in front of everyone at the ceremony. When it came to the big day, the scout leader asked the other scouts to say the promise out loud with me. This was a great idea, as speaking out loud with someone else helps me not to stutter.

One of the hardest things for me is meeting someone new. I know they say you shouldn't judge a book by its cover, but a lot of people do. When someone meets me for the first time and I sound a bit strange, they probably think I am a bit strange. This is unfair and makes me feel upset. I know I have a problem speaking, but this doesn't mean I'm stupid."

"I also find it difficult going to
the store to buy candy."

"If the store is really quiet, then I'm usually OK. If it's busy, however, and there are other people standing in line behind me, then I start to feel flustered and stutter. I know I should try to take my time, but I just want to get it over with.

I've noticed that my stutter also seems to get worse when I'm tired. Over the school vacation, I had lots of late nights, and started to stutter more than usual. Mom is usually a stickler for a regular routine and, though I hate to admit it, this is probably a good thing for me!

When I get upset about something, my stutter is really bad. The other day, I couldn't say 'yes, ma'am' when the teacher was taking attendance, and struggled talking to my best friend. I think it's because I was wound up after an argument with a friend.

Mom tries to keep everything calm at home, which helps because pressure builds up inside you when you stutter. I know she worries about me, though, and sometimes this drives me crazy. When she asks me about school, I know she wants me to tell her how my speech was, but sometimes I just don't want to talk about it. When I've had a difficult day in school, I need to relax by running around the yard or jumping on the trampoline."

"On bad days, I get really
cross with my stutter."

"It's so frustrating when you can't say what you want to say. It also makes me feel lonely. It's difficult for me to join in when other people are chatting, as by the time I've said what I want to say, everyone else has moved on.

When I'm speaking with someone who knows all about my stutter, they'll wait for me to speak and give me as much time as I need. This is really helpful, because it takes some of the pressure off me. Some people, however, try to 'help' by finishing off my sentences. This is not helpful at all, because usually they say something I wasn't going to say, and then I have to start all over again. The boy next door used to do this all the time, but since my mom explained that I need more time to speak, he doesn't interrupt so much.

I've noticed that some people look at the floor when I stutter. I think they feel uncomfortable and don't know what to do for the best. But it makes me feel like they're ignoring me. It's better when people just keep looking at me as normal. After all, I am normal—I've just got a stutter.

Joe, my best friend, is really great. It doesn't seem to bother him at all when I stutter; in fact, he hardly seems to notice. Joe just thinks of me as his best friend, not the boy with the stutter."

"Generally, recess is OK because
I like running around and playing
tag with the other children."

"At other times, I feel left out. Recently, there was a bit of a craze in school and everyone was collecting baseball cards. This meant sitting down in a huddle, telling people what cards you had, and agreeing which ones to swap. That day, I couldn't get out what I wanted to say, and the boys ignored me completely.

There have also been a few times during recess when children have started to laugh or snicker at me. They think it's funny when I stutter, but there's nothing funny about it to me. At first I didn't want to tell my teacher about this, but I'm glad I did. The bullies apologized, then, a few days later, gave me a list of famous people who stuttered just like me. (The bullies weren't allowed out at recess for two days, so I think the teacher made them do the list then.) Did you know that King George VI and Winston Churchill had stutters? And to think I thought it was just me and my brother!

It won't be long before I move up to high school. I'm not sure how I'll cope with all the different teachers there, and I'm already starting to feel quite anxious about it. This is bad because the more I worry about stuttering, the more I stutter. Mom has arranged for us to meet some of the teachers before I start, which should help make things a bit easier for me."

"As I get older, it's important for me
to speak for myself, and Mom is
really keen to encourage this."

"The other day we went out for a nice meal. I tried my best to give my order to the waitress, but she couldn't understand me and asked my mom what I wanted. Mom knew I wanted to order for myself, so she told the waitress about my stutter, and then I tried again. I still stuttered, but I did manage to give my order this time, and felt really grown up that I'd done it all by myself.

Sometimes I go to see a woman who helps me with my stutter. She's called a speech therapist and is trained to help people with all sorts of speech problems. I've been going to see her since I was quite small. Usually we play games. Not running-around games, but games with lots of talking. The speech therapist encourages me to speak slowly and smoothly, and I definitely stutter less when I'm there. Unfortunately, though, I find it hard to keep this up for long, and my stutter always comes back.

When I sit down and think about it logically, I know I would stutter less if I spoke more slowly. But because I'm so anxious to get it over and done with, I speak quickly and stumble over the words."

"I know there's no cure for stuttering, but my brother is doing really well now."

"My brother Peter is six years older than me, and has been on a few special courses to help him speak better. I don't understand it all, but he's been taught a new way of breathing. He uses this special breathing technique every time he speaks.

The techniques Peter has learned might not be suitable for everyone. Some stutterers might prefer to visit a speech therapist, rather than go away on a course. Others might prefer to talk to a counselor. I guess different things work for different people, and each stutterer has to find out what works for him or her.

Peter used to have trouble saying his name, and told me that lots of stutterers have trouble with this—not just me! Now he practices his name whenever he uses the telephone. This might not work for everyone, but it's certainly helped Peter. He can say his name fine now and has even recorded his own voice message on his cellphone."

"Peter enjoys talking about his stutter and is no longer embarrassed about it, as he was in the past."

"Peter tells people that he's learning to overcome his stutter. He's told everyone in college, and even came into my elementary school to talk about stuttering in assembly. He mentioned a special day—October 22nd—when stutterers all over the world tell people what it's like to have a stutter. This is called International Stuttering Awareness Day.

When Peter came home from his first course, he was on top of the world! But then, a few months later, he got sick with the flu, and started to stutter again. Mom said this is called a relapse. He's had to work really hard to make his speech strong again, but it's definitely worth the effort.

Mom and I help Peter by holding eye contact with him whenever he's speaking. I've noticed that Mom speaks in an unhurried way when she's around us, which is probably a good thing, as there's nothing worse for a stutterer than feeling rushed.

Most of the time Peter speaks with control, but he still gets good days and bad days, just like me. To help him see that he's making progress, Peter sets himself a new target every month. Nothing too big, but something he can definitely achieve. Mom said this might be a good idea for me too."

"Peter and I have made friends with other stutterers. They are all different and their stutters affect them in different ways."

"Peter and I know that all sorts of people, of all ages, have stutters, but it is more common in boys than girls. It's good to know that Peter and I are not alone, as it helps to support each other.

The funny thing about Peter is that lots of people didn't know he had a stutter. Everyone knows about my stutter, but Peter used tricks to hide his. When someone asked him a question, for instance, he'd always start with, 'Well, you know...' to stop him getting stuck. So, if someone asked him what he wanted for lunch, he'd say, 'Well, you know a cheese sandwich, please.' He'd even do this when saying his name: 'Well, you know Peter.' Some of his sentences didn't make much sense!

The other thing Peter would do is to change a word if he thought he was going to stutter on it and say something different instead. For example, whenever Mom went to the takeaway, Peter would have pizza. But if he had to go and ask for it himself, he would always come back with a burger. Peter doesn't really like burgers, but he'd rather eat a burger than stutter on the word 'pizza.'

Peter understands more about stuttering now and has tried to explain it to me. He used to try to cover up his stutter. (This is sometimes called a covert stutter.) In contrast, my stutter is not hidden at all. (This is sometimes called an overt stutter.)"

"Peter helps me to feel positive about the future. If he can do it, then so can I!"

"Peter knows he must not hide his stutter anymore as he needs to be open about it in order to improve his speech. He used to avoid difficult situations as well as difficult words, but not anymore! He's also given up all the tricks.

Peter says it's important not to hold back, and he's always encouraging me to try new things and give it my best. On days when my stutter is bad, it's hard not to feel down, but Peter encourages me not to dwell on things. He says we should both keep looking ahead to the future and moving forwards. Peter has a box full of positive sayings, and we start each day by reciting one out loud together. Today's was 'By perseverance, the snail reached the ark.'[1] This means we'll both get there in the end, as long as we keep trying.

Mom is really supportive of me and Peter, and I know she loves us both to bits—with or without our stutters. We know there's no quick fix to controlling a stutter, but it needn't hold us back. I hope that, over time, I learn to control my stutter, just like Peter, but I know I'll get on with my life, stutter or no stutter."

---

1 Charles Haddon Spurgeon.

How to help

"Lots of situations are difficult for me, and the more anxious I am about stuttering, the more likely I am to stutter.

When I'm speaking, it helps me if I know there's no need to rush. So please:

- give me time to think

- give me time to talk

- don't get impatient and start glancing at your watch

- don't interrupt and try to finish my sentences.

When I'm speaking, it helps me if I know that you're really listening. So please:

- maintain normal eye contact

- focus on what I'm saying rather than how I'm saying it

- don't ignore me and pretend that I'm not speaking

- don't look bored or start talking to someone else

- don't look embarrassed and stare at the floor.

Speaking in school is often difficult for me, so please:

- don't put me on the spot by firing a question at me

- ask me what works best for everyday routines such as taking attendance

- ask me if I'd like to go first when reading aloud

- ask me if I'd like to read aloud with someone else.

My stutter is usually better when I feel good about myself. So please:

- encourage me to give it a try

- praise me for things I do well

- tell me what I'm good at.

There's a lot more to me than just my stutter, so please:

- don't label me

- focus on me as a person, with strengths and weaknesses just like everyone else

- give me the same opportunities as everyone else

- don't assume I'm less intelligent just because I stutter

- don't make fun of me.

Using the telephone can be scary for me, so please:

- give me the opportunity to make and receive calls, and record a voicemail, if I want to

- help me to keep focused by maintaining eye contact.

After a busy day at school, I need some time to chill and relax. So please:

- don't bombard me with lots of questions the minute I come in

- show interest in how my day went, but not just in my speech

- help me to stick to a routine, eat well, and get enough sleep.

It's far better for me to try speaking and stutter, than not to speak at all. So please:

- encourage me to speak in different situations

- encourage me to practice difficult words

- don't speak for me.

Living with a stutter takes bravery and courage. So please encourage me:

- to be open and honest about my stutter

- not to hold back

- not to use tricks to hide my stutter.

Many people succeed in learning how to control their stutters. I know this will be very hard work and will take a lot of effort and discipline. So please:

- support me as I learn to overcome my stutter

- remind me to use the techniques
  I learn every time I speak

- encourage me to set small, achievable
  targets to keep me motivated

- encourage me to be proud of who I am."

Recommended reading, websites, and organizations

If you would like to find out more about stuttering, here are some useful books, organizations, and websites.

BOOKS

Byrne, R. and Wright, L. (2008) *Stammering: Advice for All Ages*. London: Sheldon Press.

Kelman, E. and Nicholas, A. (2008) *Practical Intervention for Early Childhood Stammering*. Milton Keynes: Speechmark Publishing.

Kelman, E. and Whyte, A. (2012) *Understanding Stammering or Stuttering*. London: Jessica Kingsley Publishers.

McGuire, D. (2002) *Beyond Stammering: The McGuire Programme for Getting Good at the Sport of Speaking*. London: Souvenir Press.

O'Shea, M. (2007) *Why I Called My Sister Harry*. Bloomington, IN: Trafford Publishing.

ORGANIZATIONS AND WEBSITES

USA

Friends: The National Association of Young People who Stutter
38 South Oyster Bay Rd.
Syosset, NY 11791

Phone: 866 866 8335
Email: LCAGGIANO@aol.com
Website: www.friendswhostutter.org

National Stuttering Association
119 W 40th Street, 14th Floor
New York, NY 10018
Phone: 212 944 4050
Email: info@WeStutter.org
Website: www.nsastutter.org

The Stuttering Foundation
P.O. Box 11749
Memphis, TN 38111–0749
Phone: (800) 992 9392 or (901) 761 0343
Email: info@stutteringhelp.org
Website: www.stutteringhelp.org

The Stuttering Homepage
www.stutteringhomepage.com

UK

British Stammering Association
15 Old Ford Road
London
E2 9PJ
Phone: 020 8983 1003
Email: mail@stammering.org
Website: www.stammering.org

City Lit
Keeley Street
Covent Garden
London
WC2B 4BA
Phone: 020 7492 2600
Email: infoline@citylit.ac.uk
Website: www.citylit.ac.uk/courses/speech_therapy

City University London
Northampton Square
London
EC1V 0HB
Phone: 020 7040 5060
Email: enquiries@city.ac.uk
Website: www.city.ac.uk/health/public-clinics/compass-centre/
stammering-clinic

Royal College of Speech and Language Therapists
2 White Hart Yard
London
SE1 1NX
Phone (main switchboard): 020 7378 1200
Phone (general information): 020 7378 3012
Email: info@rcslt.org
Website: www.rcslt.org

The Fluency Trust
West Swindon Health Centre
Link Avenue
Swindon
SN5 7DL
Phone: 01793 877233
Website: www.thefluencytrust.org.uk

The Michael Palin Centre for Stammering Children
13–15 Pine Street
London
EC1R 0JG
Phone: 020 3316 8100
Website: www.stammeringcentre.org

The Stammering Support Centre
Leeds Community Healthcare NHS Trust
First Floor, Stockdale House
Headingley Office Park
Victoria Road
Leeds
LS6 1PF

Phone: 0113 220 8500
Website: www.leedscommunityhealthcare.nhs.uk/
stammeringsupportcentre

UCL Psychology and Language Sciences
Speech Research Group
Department of Cognitive, Perceptual and Brain Sciences
University College London
26 Bedford Way, Room 441
London
WC1 0AP
Phone: 0207 679 7566
Website: www.ucl.ac.uk/speech-research-group

Republic of Ireland
Michael O'Shea
Website: www.michaeloshea.ie

Australia
Australian Speak Easy Association
PO Box 5342
West End
Queensland 4101
Website: www.speakeasy.org.au

South Africa
Speak Easy South Africa
Phone: 082 820 6225
Email: info@speakeasy.org.za
Website: www.speakeasy.org.za

Europe
The European League of Stuttering Associations
www.stuttering.ws

International

International Stuttering Association

c/o Joseph Lukong Tardzenyuy (Secretary)
1018 South Payne Street
New Ulm, MN 56073
USA
Email: admin@isastutter.org
Website: www.stutterisa.org

The McGuire Programme

Email: dave@mcguireprogramme.com
Website: www.mcguireprogramme.com

Blank, for your notes

Blank, for your drawings